Catholic

Prayers

to

Saintly

Germanic

Kings & Queens

Catholic Prayers to Saintly Germanic Kings & Queens

BY **MARIE NOËL**

ADAPTED & COMPILED FROM
APPROVED SOURCES

BOOKSBYNOËL.COM

Catholic Prayers to Saintly Germanic Kings &
Queens

ISBN-13: 978-0-9893310-1-2

Translations by Marie Noël

Interior design & typesetting: Renata L. Reyez
Graphic design by Ariel
Cover image: "Founding of an abbey by
St. Richardis" (circa 1840). Courtesy Wikimedia
Commons

BooksByNoël.com

First Edition

Contents

Introduction

This is the 2nd collection in a series of prayers to holy Catholic kings and queens. It follows "Catholic Prayers to the King & Queen of Heaven with Prayers for the Kings & Queens on Earth."

Most prayers are translated from other languages. Many date back to the Middle Ages and include saints popular during that time.

This collection primarily focuses on Germanic saints. The creation of this book involved much research as it was necessary to find these saints, verify they indeed were saints recognized by the Catholic

Church, search for Catholic prayers to/about them, and, finally, locate images.

Another challenge included how to group them since the borders of European countries changed throughout history. Some countries where these saints once ruled no longer exist today. Also, some saints were born in faraway nations but became patrons of Germanic lands.

Additionally included are sections of prayers for the peoples of the countries represented. I enjoyed creating this collection. I traveled back and forth in time to distant lands while learning about heroic virtue. Both the cultures and saints of these nations are truly inspiring.

I would like to specially acknowledge the Papal Swiss Guards for providing me with a prayer.

"Christch triumphing over death and sin" by
Peter Paul Rubens (1615). Courtesy Wikimedia
Commons.

Chapter 1:
Christ the King

Prayers to Jesus

"The Sacred Heart of Jesus" by unknown.

Holy Mass for the Solemnity of Christ the King

The Truth of Christ is to be preached in all times and seasons, in all places and circumstances. It is to be preached in humility and powerlessness, as an invitation for all to enter into that Kingdom where the King of Love reigns over hearts and minds. It is a Kingdom that comes when the will of the individual is conformed to the will of God; it begins here on earth and finds its fulfillment in Heaven.

Archbishop Gerhard Ludwig Müller, Nov. 25, 2012

To Jesus Christ, the King

O Christ Jesus, I acknowledge you as universal King. All that has been made was created for you. Exercise over me all your sovereign rights. I renew my baptismal promises, renouncing Satan, his pomps and his works, and I promise to live as a good Christian. Especially do I pledge myself, by all the means in my power, to bring about the triumphs of the rights of God and of your Church.

Divine heart of Jesus, I consecrate all my poor actions to the cause of your Kingship, that all hearts may recognize you their ruler and thus establish the kingdom of your peace in all the world. Amen.

Prayer to
Christ the King

Feast Day:
Last Sunday of October

Almighty and everlasting God, after you created Heaven and earth, and all the living beings, plants and animals, then you created man.

You made him king of your whole creation. You put everything in the whole world at his disposal. You gave to him alone, of all the creatures on this earth, the power to think and the power to will.

Everything else was made to serve man. Then, when man sinned, you sent your son to be the King of mankind, and the Redeemer of the human race.

He is now King, not only of mankind, but of the whole universe. He is the "firstborn of every creature." He is our King, and everything that we have is made and given us to serve him. We are to use it, not in selfishness and greed, but in gratitude and generosity, realizing that we are all subjects of the great King Jesus.

Help us to keep this in mind, as we plough his fields

loaned to us for a time, and as we reap his crops, given to us by his generous hand. Help us to use with care the goods he here gives us, so that we may gain the eternal goods that he has won for us.

Help us always and everywhere to be good, loyal subjects of Christ, our King, so that we may be with him, our victor and King, forever in Heaven. *Amen.*

*"Jesus Christ the King surrounded by angels"
by Hans Memling (circa 1489). Courtesy
Wikimedia Commons.*

Hail, Christ Our King

Most sweet Jesus, come near to us, your children. Receive from our hands that crown which those who are but dust of earth try to seize from you. Enter now in triumph among us, your fervent followers.

- *Hail, Christ our King!*

Lawmakers may break the tables of your law, but while they lose their thrones and are forgotten, we, your subjects, will continue to salute you.

- *Hail, Christ our King!*

They have said that your Gospel is out-of-date, that it hinders progress, and must no longer be considered. They who say this soon disappear into obscurity and are forgotten; while we, who adore you, continue to salute you.

- *Hail, Christ our King!*

The proud, the worldly, those who possess unlawful riches, those who thirst for riches, honors and pleasures alone, declaring your moral law to be for past ages, will be hurled against the rock of Calvary and your Church and falling, will be reduced to dust, and sink into oblivion, while we, your followers, continue to salute you.

- *Hail, Christ our King!*

Those who seek the dawn of a material civilization, divorced from God, will surely die, poisoned by their own false doctrine, deserted and cursed by their own children, while we, who would console you, will continue to salute you.

• *Hail, Christ our King!*

Yes, hail to you, O Christ, our King! Put to flight Lucifer, the fallen angel of darkness, from our homes, schools and society, force him and his agents into hell, chain him there everlastingly, while we, your friends, continue to salute you.

• *Hail, Christ our King!*

"Ecce Homo" by Guido Reni (circa 1640).
Courtesy Wikimedia Commons.

Feast Honoring the Crown of Our Lord

(St. Louis instituted this feast Aug. 11, 1239 after receiving a relic of the Crown of Thorns. Other Crown of Thorns feast days followed: 2nd Friday of March, April 24, the Friday after Ash Wednesday & May 4.)

Let us all rejoice in the Lord, who celebrate the feast in honor of the crown of the Lord, on which angels rejoice and praise the Son of God. Angels rejoice, and archangels are glad; and all the saints are joyful and full of mirth.

Grant, we ask you, Almighty God, that we, who in memory of the passion of our Lord Jesus Christ, adore upon earth his Crown of Thorns, may be worthy to be crowned by him with honor and glory in Heaven.

• *Alleluia! We reverence your crown, O Lord. We celebrate your glorious triumph.*

• *Alleluia! A Crown of Thorns this day we venerate by which is won a wreath of glorious state.*

Strengthen, O Almighty King, the valor of your soldiers, that they, who in the conflicts of this mortal life are cheered by the crown of your only-begotten Son, may, after they have finished their course, receive the prize of immortality. We humbly ask you, Almighty God, that the feast which we celebrate will amend and profit us by virtue of the holy crown of your Son. Through Christ our Lord. *Amen.*

"Immaculate Conception" (circa 1600s). By unknown. Courtesy Wikimedia Commons.

Chapter 2:

Mary, Queen of Heaven

Prayers to the Blessed Virgin Mary

Through the Virgin Mary let us turn with trust to the One who rules the world and holds in his hand the future of the universe.

For centuries she has been invoked as the celestial Queen of Heaven; in the *Litany of Loreto* after the prayer of the holy Rosary, she is implored 8 times: as Queen of Angels, of Patriarchs, of Prophets, of Apostles, of Martyrs, of Confessors, of Virgins, of all the Saints and of Families.

The rhythm of these ancient invocations and daily prayers, such as the *Salve Regina,* help us to understand that the Blessed Virgin, as our Mother beside her Son Jesus in the glory of Heaven, is always with us in the daily events of our life.

The title "Queen" is thus a title of trust, joy and love. And we know that the One who holds a part of the world's destinies in her hand is good, that she loves us and helps us in our difficulties.

Pope Benedict XVI, Aug. 22, 2012

Regina Coeli

O Queen of Heaven, rejoice. Alleluia. For he whom you were worthy to bear. Alleluia. Has arisen, as he said. Alleluia. Pray for us to God. Alleluia.

• *Rejoice and be glad, O Virgin Mary. Alleluia.*

• *For the Lord has risen indeed. Alleluia.*

Let Us Pray

O God, who gave joy to the world through the resurrection of your son, our Lord Jesus Christ, grant we ask you, through the intercession of the Virgin Mary, his mother, we may obtain the joys of everlasting life. Through the same Christ our Lord. *Amen.*

Hail Holy Queen

Hail, Holy Queen, mother of mercy, our life, our sweetness, and our hope. To you do we cry, poor banished children of Eve. To you do we send up our sighs, mourning and weeping in this valley of tears. Turn then, our most gracious advocate, your eyes of mercy towards us, and after this our exile, show to us the blessed fruit of your womb, Jesus.

O clement, O loving, O sweet Virgin Mary. Pray for us, O Holy Mother of God, that we may be made worthy of the promises of Christ of Lord. *Amen.*

"*Coronation of the Virgin Mary*" *by Jean Fouquet
(circa 1400s). Courtesy Wikimedia Commons.*

To Mary, Queen of Heaven & Mistress of the World

(from the 1800s)

Holy Mary, Queen of Heaven, mother of our Lord Jesus Christ, and mistress of the world, who forsakes no one and despises no one.

Look upon me, O Lady with an eye of pity and ask your beloved Son on my behalf for the forgiveness of all my sins; that as I recall with devout affection your holy and Immaculate Conception, so, hereafter, I may receive the prize of eternal blessedness, by the grace of Him whom you, in virginity, did bring forth, Jesus Christ our Lord.

Who, with the Father and the Holy Ghost, lives and reigns, in perfect Trinity, one God, world without end. *Amen.*

To Mary, the Queen of Mercy

(by St. Alphonsus Liguori 1696-1787)

O Queen and mother of mercy, who dispenses graces to all who have recourse to you with so much generosity because you are a queen, and with so much love because you are our most loving Mother.

To you do I, who so lack in merit and virtue, and am so loaded with debts to the divine justice, recommend myself this day.

O Mary, you hold the keys of all the divine mercies.

"*Coronation of the Virgin Mary*" *by Maître
François (circa 1460). Courtesy The British
Library.*

Don't forget my miseries and leave me in my poverty. You are so generous with all, and give more than you are asked for. Oh be generous with me.

O Lady, protect me, this is all I ask of you. If you protect me, I fear nothing. I fear not the evil spirits for you are more powerful than all of them. I fear not my sins for you by one word can obtain their full pardon from God.

And if I have your favor, I do not even fear an angry God since a single prayer of yours will appease him. Therefore, if you protect me, I place all my hope in you since you are all powerful.

O Mother of mercy, I know you take pleasure in helping the most miserable (as long as they are not obstinate) and I know that you can indeed help them. I am a sinner, but I'm not obstinate.

I desire to change my life. You can then help me. Oh help me and save me.

I now place myself entirely in your hands. Tell me what I must do in order to please God, and I am ready for all, and hope to do all with your help, O Mary, my Mother, my light, my consolation, my refuge, and my hope. *Amen.*

"Mater Dolorosa" by Carlo Dolci (circa 1650).

Queen of Sorrows

(translated from 1800s

German prayer)

O Mary, dolorous mother, remember the sorrows which you did suffer at the foot of the cross of your Son, and have mercy on us sinners.

Assist us in life, and take us under your protection in the hour of death that we may persevere in the grace of God and be saved. *Amen.*

To Mary, Queen of Love

(by St. Alphonsus)

Mary, Queen of Love, of all creatures the most amiable, the most beloved, and the most loving, my own sweet mother.

You were always and in all things inflamed with love towards God; deign then to bestow, at least, a spark of it on me.

You did pray to your Son for the spouses whose wine had failed: 'They have no wine.'

And will you not pray for us, in whom the love of God, whom we are under such obligations to love, is wanting.

Just say also, 'They have no love,' and obtain us this love.

This is the only grace for which we ask. O Mother, by the love you bear for Jesus, graciously hear and pray for us. *Amen.*

*Blessed Karl of Austria, Emperor & Apostolic
King of Hungary*

Chapter 3: Austria

Royal Austrian Saints

The decisive task of Christians consists in seeking, recognizing and following God's will in all things. The Christian statesman, Charles of Austria, confronted this challenge every day.

To his eyes, war appeared as "something appalling." Amid the tumult of the First World War, he strove to promote the peace initiative of my Predecessor, Benedict XV.

From the beginning, the Emperor Charles conceived of his office as a holy service to his people. His chief concern was to follow the Christian vocation to holiness also in his political actions. For this reason, his thoughts turned to social assistance.

May he be an example for all of us, especially for those who have political responsibilities in Europe today!

Pope John Paul II, October 2004

"Archduchess Elizabeth of Austria, Queen of France, in Mourning" by Jakob de Monte (circa 1580). Courtesy Wikimedia Commons.

To All Saints of the Three Orders of St. Francis

O God, the protector of all who trust in you, without whom nothing is strong and nothing is holy, we ask you to multiply upon us your mercy: that you being our ruler, you our guide, we may so pass through temporal good things so as not to lose those that are eternal. Amen.

"*Elizabeth of Austria, Queen Consort of Charles
IX of France*" *by Georges van der Straeten
(1573). Courtesy The Yourck Project.*

Elizabeth of Austria, Servant of God

(1554-1592)

Feast Day: December 20

• *Queen of France, wife of King Charles IX.*

• *Daughter of Holy Roman Emperor Maximilian II of Austria & Infanta Maria of Spain.*

• *Married at 15, widowed 4 years later.*

• *She shunned royal life & refused a second marriage. She joined the Third Order of St. Francis, taking vows & following his rule of poverty, prayer and penance.*

• She dedicated her time and resources to prayer and serving the poor. She founded a convent for Poor Clares, restored a chapel in Prague, and spent her money on the poor and needy.

To Elizabeth of Austria

O Blessed Elizabeth of Austria, glorious citizen of Heaven, as I give my most humble thanks to God for all the good he has done for you.

I ask you to remember me in your prayers, and to obtain for me the entire pardon of my sins, the amendment of my life, and the imitation of your good spirit and holy graces, that I may be reconciled to my Savior and always please him.

But especially I recommend to you the hour of my death that, by your holy intercession, my soul may depart from this world in the grace of God, and may immediately come to everlasting life. *Amen.*

Blessed Karl of Austria, Emperor & Apostolic King of Hungary

(1887-1922)

Feast Day: October 21

- *Also called Charles I of Austria*
- *Son of Archduke Otto of Austria & Princess Maria Josepha of Saxony.*
- *Married Zita of Bourbon-Parma in 1911. They had 8 children. He is noted for having told her on his deathbed,*

"I'll love you forever."

- *Proclaimed Emperor of Austria & King of Hungary in 1916 after assassination of his uncle.*

- *A peace-loving & devout Catholic, he tried to bring about peace during World War I.*

- *Two years later, the Austro-Hungarian Empire fell; he was forced to resign but refused to abdicate since he considered his duty a mandate from God.*

- *He was forced into exile on a remote isle in Portugal to live in poverty with his family, where he died of complications from the flu.*

For Blessed Karl's Intercession

O Blessed Emperor Karl, you accepted the difficult tasks and burdensome challenges that God gave you during your life. In every thought, decision and action you trusted always in the Holy Trinity.

We pray to you to intercede for us with the Lord our God to give us faith and courage, so that even in the most difficult situations of our earthly lives we may not lose heart, but continue faithfully in the footsteps of Christ. Ask for us the grace that our hearts may be molded into the likeness of the Sacred Heart of Jesus.

Help us to work with compassion and strength for the poor and needy, to fight with courage for peace in our homes and in the world, and in every situation to trustingly place our lives in the hands of God, until we reach Him, as you did, through Christ our Lord. *Amen.*

From the Vatican for the 2004 Beatification of Charles of Austria

Charles envisaged this office also as a way to follow Christ: in the love and care of the peoples entrusted to him, and in dedicating his life to them. He placed the most sacred duty of a king - a commitment to peace - at the center of his preoccupations during the course of the terrible war. He was the only one among political leaders to support Benedict XV's peace efforts. As far as domestic politics are concerned, despite the extremely difficult times he initiated wide and exemplary social legislation, inspired by social Christian teaching. Thanks to his conduct, the transition to a new order at the end of the conflict was made possible without a civil war. He was however banished from his country.

Prayer to God for the Faith of Blessed Emperor Karl

God Our Father, through the gift of Blessed Emperor Karl you have given us an example to follow. In extremely difficult times he performed his burdensome tasks without ever losing his faith. He always followed your Son, the true king.

He led a humble life, sincerely loving the poor and giving himself heart and soul to the search for peace. Even when his life was in danger he trusted in you, putting his life in your hands. Almighty and merciful God, by the intercession of Blessed Emperor Karl, we pray that you may give us his unconditional faith to support us in our most difficult situations, and the courage to always follow the example of your only Son.

Open our hearts to the poor, and strengthen our commitment for peace within our families and among all peoples. We ask this through Christ our Lord. *Amen.*

"*Founding of an abbey by St. Richardis*" *(circa 1840). Courtesy Wikimedia Commons.*

St. Richardis, Holy Roman Empress

(839-895 A.D.)

Feast Day: September 18

• *Also called Richarde, Richarda & Richardis of Swabia.*

• **Daughter of Kenneth I, a** *Scottish emigre and Count of Alsace & Princess Maria Josepha of Saxony.*

• *At age 22 married Charles II (Charles the Fat) and founded a convent where she stayed to seek refuge after much neglect by her husband. She filled her life with works for the church and in prayer.*

• *After many years of an unconsummated marriage, Charles falsely accused her of infidelity. A "trial by fire" was ordered.*

• *Spending hours in prayer, she repeated: "Lord, I am innocent, you will deliver me not to my slanderers!" Afterwards, she clad herself in a white garment soaked in wax, and held a cross close to her heart. Despite a fire being built around her and passing over hot coals, she wasn't burned - proving her innocence. For hundreds of years, the white garment was displayed in an abbey of Saint-Pierre Etival in France.*

• *After her ordeal, she announced that she was leaving her husband and consecrated herself to Christ. She left to establish a Benedictine abbey in Andlau, Germany, where she wrote articles in the abbey dedicated to Jesus the Savior.*

• She is invoked for protection against fires. One of her emblems is a bear in honor of one that scratched the ground to point out where she should build Andlau Abbey in Alsace.

"*Queen praying at Mass*" *by unknown (circa mid-1300s). Courtesy The British Library.*

Ancient Litany of St. Richardis

Lord have mercy on us.

Christ have mercy on us.

Lord have mercy on us.

Christ hear us.

Christ graciously hear us.

God the Father of Heaven, *have mercy on us.*

God the Son, Redeemer of the world, *have mercy on us.*

God the Holy Spirit, *have mercy on us.*

Holy Trinity, one God, *have mercy on us.*

Holy Mary, *pray for us.*

Holy Mother of God, *pray for us.*

Saint Richarde, born of royal blood, *pray for us.*

Vessel of divine grace, *pray for us.*

Vessel of love and fear of God, *pray for us.*

Vessel of faith and hope, *pray for us.*

Vessel of infinite virtues, *pray for us.*

Glory of kings and princes, *pray for us.*

Ornament of Alsace, *pray for us.*

Honor of the nobility, *pray for us.*

Mirror of true devotion, *pray for us.*

Mirror of patience, *pray for us.*

Mirror of purity, *pray for us.*

Mirror of patience, *pray for us.*

Mirror of charity, *pray for us.*

Virgin most strong, *pray for us.*

Virgin most merciful, *pray for us.*

Virgin most courteous, *pray for us.*

Virgin most cautious, *pray for us.*

Mother of the poor, *pray for us.*

Founding houses of God, *pray for us.*

You who increased the number of God's servants, *pray for us.*

You who venerate the clergy, *pray for us.*

You who promote Catholic churches and love the cross of Christ, *pray for us.*

You who vanquish demons, *pray for us.*

You who love peace, *pray for us.*

Pillar of loyalty, *pray for us.*

Vessel of triple purity, *pray for us.*

You who suffered ignominies, *pray for us.*

You who forgave those who offended you, *pray for us.*

You who loved your enemies, *pray for us.*

Model of wives, *pray for us.*

Mother of widows, *pray for us.*

Ornament of virgins, *pray for us.*

Comforter of the afflicted and persecuted, *pray for us.*

Companion of pilgrims, *pray for us.*

Cure of the sick, *pray for us.*

Health of the lowly, *pray for us.*

Rescuer of those who implore you in all their needs, *pray for us.*

Help of Christians, *pray for us.*

Refuge of sinners, *pray for us.*

Joy of the angels, *pray for us.*

Glory of the saints, *pray for us.*

Beloved intercessor for us, *pray for us.*

From all evil, *deliver us, O Lord.*

From all sin, *deliver us, O Lord.*

From any danger of sin, *deliver us, O Lord.*

From suspicion, *deliver us, O Lord.*

From false accusations and slander, *deliver us, O Lord.*

From ignoring our conscience, *deliver us, O Lord.*

From bad thoughts and unbridled passions, *deliver us, O Lord.*

From cruel temptations, *deliver us, O Lord.*

From anger, hatred and all ill will,

deliver us, O Lord.

From disunity and discord, *deliver us, O Lord.*

From disgust and negligence in the service of God, *deliver us, O Lord.*

From any irregularity of life, *deliver us, O Lord.*

From famine, war, pestilence, and any disease, *deliver us, O Lord.*

From all the dangers of life, *deliver us, O Lord.*

From the eternal fire of hell, *deliver us, O Lord.*

Through the merits and intercession of the Holy Empress Richardis, *deliver us, O Lord.*

Through the devotion and virtues with which the princess shone over all the earth, *deliver us, O Lord.*

By the fidelity with which she

showed in Heaven and with her earthly husband, *deliver us, O Lord.*

By the fear that surprised your servant when the chaste virgin was publicly accused of the most horrific crime of adultery, *deliver us, O Lord.*

By patience, meekness and humility that carried this Princess when she appeared in court, as a sinner, in flames, dressed in a waxed garment, *deliver us, O Lord.*

By fervent prayer that your servant made at the Abbey in Andlau, *deliver us, O Lord.*

By many visions in which you honored, consoled and instructed Holy Richardis, *deliver us, O Lord.*

By holy zeal with which your servant brought the church in your honor and in honor of your Apostles, *deliver us, O Lord.*

By the divine will in which you

raised the Holy Empress with merits and had the bear scratch the soil to point out in a miraculous way that the Valley Andlau was the best place to build your church, *deliver us, O Lord.*

By the infinite love and foresight you showed to humanity in your incarnation and your birth, *deliver us, O Lord.*

For the love that you were wrapped in swaddling clothes on the day of your birth and childhood, *deliver us, O Lord.*

For the love that you delivered yourself into the hands of your enemies, *deliver us, O Lord.*

By your deliverance to the judge, *deliver us, O Lord.*

For the links and ropes with which you were attached to the column to be scourged, *deliver us, O Lord.*

By your Cross and Passion, *deliver us, O Lord.*

By the nails with which you were attached to the Cross, *deliver us, O Lord.*

By shroud in which you were placed in the tomb when your body was detached from the cross, *deliver us, O Lord.*

By the innocence of the Holy Queen and Empress Richardis, who was persecuted for Christ, we who are sinners ask, *deliver us, O Lord.*

Forgive us, we beseech you, *hear us.*

For you to help us in our own spiritual and physical difficulties through the merits and intercession of the Holy Empress Richardis, *we beseech you, hear us.*

For you to arouse in us a true zeal and devotion to the true service of

God, *we beseech you, hear us.*

For you to give troubled souls true peace of heart and to unite everyone to the will of God, *we beseech you, hear us.*

For you to keep all the virgins and widows in purity according to their condition, *we beseech you, hear us.*

For you bless all Christian spouses with unity and patience, *we beseech you, hear us.*

For you to protect us in our dangers and at the hour of our death, *we beseech you, hear us.*

For you to provide us true Christian patience with our cross and persecutions, *we beseech you, hear us.*

For you to provide us with final perseverance, *we beseech you, hear us.*

Lamb of God, who takes away the sins of the world, through the intercession of St. Richardis, *hear us.*

Lamb of God, who takes away the sins of the world, *spare us.*

Lamb of God, who takes away the sins of the world, *have mercy on us.*

Let Us Pray

O God, who kept Holy Richardis pure, grant us the grace to reach you with a chaste heart, through the intercession and merits of one who, in the state of marriage, deserved and obtained the crown of a virgin. So be it. *Amen.*

Austria's Patron Saints

"St. Leopold III, Margrave" by Wilhelm August Rieder (1849). Courtesy Wikimedia Commons.

Novena to St. Leopold, Patron of Austria

O God, who governs all things, you granted to the holy Margrave Leopold the gifts of your Spirit for service to the Holy Church, for the just exercise of his office, and for fidelity to his family.

Through his intercession, grant us the grace to remain true to the Church and to our God-given obligations, and the wisdom to recognize your Spirit in the world.

Grant moreover, O merciful Father, by St. Leopold's intercession, the request we now mention (____). We ask this through Christ Our Lord. Amen.

To Our Lady of Mariazell

Holy Mary, Immaculate Mother of our Lord Jesus Christ, in you God has given us the model of the Church and of genuine humanity.

To you I entrust the country of Austria and its people.

Help all of us to follow your example and to direct our lives completely to God! Grant that, by looking to Christ, we may become ever more like him: true children of God!

Then we too, filled with every spiritual blessing, will be able to conform ourselves more fully to his will and to become instruments of his peace for Austria, Europe and the world. *Amen.*

(by Pope Benedict XVI at the Shrine of Mariazell, 2007)

"*St. Florian*" *by Anton Cebej (circa 1765).*
Courtesy Wikimedia Commons.

Litany to St. Florian, Patron of Austria

Lord have mercy upon us.

Christ have mercy upon us.

Holy Mary, pray for us.

St. Florian, courageous soldier of Christ, *pray for us.*

St. Florian, unconquered martyr of Christ, *pray for us.*

St. Florian, despiser of the world, *pray for us.*

St. Florian, mirror and pattern of soldiers, *pray for us.*

St. Florian, ornament of Austria, *pray for us.*

St. Florian, valiant captain, *pray for us.*

St. Florian, who, on account of the

successes of your 40 soldiers, were full of cures, *pray for us.*

St. Florian, who brought your comrades to martyrdom by your exhortations, *pray for us.*

St. Florian, who offered yourself to the governor Aquilino, *pray for us.*

St. Florian, who offered yourself to death for Christ, and willingly bore it, *pray for us.*

St. Florian, who confessed the faith of Christ with loud voice, *pray for us.*

St. Florian, who, for this confession, was slain, *pray for us.*

St. Florian, whose shoulders were branded and lacerated with hot irons, *pray for us.*

St. Florian, who remained steadfast in the faith under most dreadful suffering, *pray for us.*

St. Florian, who with bound hands and feet, had millstones tied around your neck while thrown into the Enns river, *pray for us.*

St. Florian, who passing through fire and water entered the land of eternal life, *pray for us.*

St. Florian, who was crowned in Heaven, *pray for us.*

St. Florian, who in the presence of God will bloom to all eternity, *pray for us.*

St. Florian, whose body was by an unseen power saved from the river, and deposited on a rock, *pray for us.*

St. Florian, whose body an eagle protected and showed to the Christians, *pray for us.*

St. Florian, who was taken and buried by Valeria and other pious women, *pray for us.*

St. Florian, who by a miraculous

spring of water refreshed the oxen who were half dead from lack of water, while conveying your holy body to the grave, *pray for us.*

St. Florian, who obtained from God for this well such powers that the sick were healed by it, *pray for us.*

St. Florian, who after your burial did immediately raise the dead body of another to life, *pray for us.*

St. Florian, who when invoked by a man who had fallen on burning coals, restored him uninjured, *pray for us.*

St. Florian, you powerful protector against fire, *pray for us.*

Lamb of God that takes away the sin of the world, *spare us, O Lord.*

• *Our Father, who art in Heaven, hallowed be thy Name, thy kingdom come, thy will be done, on earth as it is in Heaven. Give us this day our daily bread, and forgive us our trespasses, as we forgive those who trespass against us. And lead us not into temptation, but deliver us from evil. Amen.*

• *Hail Mary, full of grace, the Lord is with thee: blessed art thou among women, and blessed is the fruit of thy womb, Jesus. Holy Mary, mother of God, pray for us sinners, now and at the hour of our death. Amen.*

• *Glory be to the Father and to the Son and to the Holy Spirit. As it was in the beginning is now, and ever shall be, world without end. Amen.*

O Holy Florian, valiant champion of Christ, who left your honorable career of arms to give yourself for the sake of the faith to such cruel martyrdom and torment, recommend us to the Lord our God.

Pray for us, O Holy Martyr Florian, that we may be graciously preserved from the effect of fire.

Most glorious martyr of Christ, Holy Florian, who remained so constant and unmoved in faith and love, that no flattery of words or torments could turn you from the true service of God.

We implore you with great humility that you through your great merits and intercession would obtain for us from the most gracious God, help in trouble, consolation in persecution, refreshment in difficulties, and support in temptations, that we may perceive all the evils of the devil, that we may escape his snares, that we may fly from the sins of the world, that we may despise worldly honors, that we may fear no opposition, that we may overcome the temptations of the flesh, that we may constantly practice virtue, and lastly, through your intercession obtain and enjoy eternal happiness and blessedness.

Jesus, Maria, Joseph, Joachim, Ann, and the Most Holy Sacrament of the Altar, be our consolation now and at the hour of our death. *Amen.*

"Henry crowned Holy Roman Emperor" (circa 1400-1410). Courtesy Wikimedia Commons.

Chapter 4:

Germany

Royal German Saints

Again and again the very notion of saints has been caricatured and distorted, as if to be holy meant to be remote from the world, naive and joyless.

Often it is thought that a saint has to be someone with great ascetic and moral achievements, who might well be revered, but could never be imitated in our own lives.

How false and discouraging this opinion is!

There is no saint, apart from the Blessed Virgin Mary, who has not also known sin, who has never fallen. ... Christ is not so much interested in how often in our lives we stumble and fall, as in how often with his help we pick ourselves up again.

He does not demand glittering achievements, but he wants his light to shine in you.

He does not call you because you are good and perfect, but because he is good and he wants to make you his friends.

Yes, you are the light of the world because Jesus is your light.

You are Christians – not because you do special and extraordinary things, but because he, Christ, is your life, our life.

You are holy, we are holy, if we allow his grace to work in us.

Pope Benedict XVI, Sept. 24, 2011

"St. Benedict with St. Radegund" by unknown (1450). Courtesy Wikimedia Commons.

For St. Radegund's Help

O God, who by your mercy, were anxious to withdraw the soul of the holy St. Radegund from life into Heaven. Through her intercession, grant to us your servants, who remain here below on our earthly pilgrimage, the grace not to be corrupted by the evil of this world, nor seduced by its illusions. We ask you this through Jesus Christ our Lord. Amen.

St. Radegund, German Princess & Queen of France

(520-580 A.D.)

Feast Day: August 13

• *Born a princess of Thuringia, she is also known as Radegonde, Radegunde, Radegundis & Radegunda.*

• *Daughter of Queen Clothaire & King Berthaire. Her two paternal uncles were German kings.*

• *Radegund was taken at an early age to live with her uncle after he murdered her father. That same uncle later slayed his other brother in a conspiracy with the Franks. At age 11, she was taken prisoner by Clothar I, king of the Franks, after he killed her remaining uncle in a raid on her homeland. She then was educated in the French court and baptized by St. Medard, bishop of Noyon. She became very devoted to her faith and prayer life & consecrated herself to God.*

• At age 19 she fled the court when King Clothar wanted to marry her, but was arrested & taken back. She became Queen upon marriage. Six years later, the French king murdered her brother to get the territory in Thuringia. She ran away & St. Medard convinced the king to allow her to fulfill her wish to lead a monastic life.

• *She eventually built the Convent of the Holy Cross in Poitiers with land donated by the king & lived a virtuous life. St. Gregory of Tours wrote her biography.*

"St. Venantius Fortunatus reading his poems to St. Radegund" by Lawrence Alma-Tadema (1862). Courtesy Wikimedia Commons.

Litany of St. Radegund

(translated from French)

Lord God, Father in Heaven, *have mercy on us.*

Lord God, Son and Redeemer of the world, *have mercy on us.*

Lord God, the Holy Spirit, *have mercy on us.*

Holy Trinity, one God, *have mercy on us.*

Holy Mary, mother of God, *have mercy on us.*

St. Radegund, *pray for us.*

You who belong to the people that

God has ransomed, *pray for us.*

You who God chose for his glorious service, *pray for us.*

You who have served God and others with a humble and gentle heart, *pray for us.*

You who realized the value of higher rewards, *pray for us.*

You who used your power in the service of good, *pray for us.*

You whose heart glowed with charity in a torn world, *pray for us.*

You who abandoned everything for a heavenly pearl without a price, *pray for us.*

You who Christ views as a jewel in his crown, *pray for us.*

You who contemplated the invisible, *pray for us.*

You who understood the cross of Jesus, *pray for us.*

You who on Earth already lived among the company of the saints, *pray for us.*

You who thought incessantly of the poor and the weak, *pray for us.*

You who were able to loosen the bonds of wickedness, *pray for us.*

You who prayed for enlightenment for your husband, *pray for us.*

You whose faith studied deeply of the things of God, *pray for us.*

You who the Lord revealed the secrets he saves for his friends, *pray for us.*

You who were filled completely by Christ, *pray for us.*

You who by your prayer attracted around you the blessings God, *pray for us.*

You who triumphed over evil, *pray for us.*

You who have gave hope to those who are lost, *pray for us.*

You who learned that it is good to wait quietly for the salvation of God, *pray for us.*

You who were filled with joy by the holy sacrament of the altar, *pray for us.*

You who for centuries have been the ideal model of consecrated life, *pray for us.*

You who lend your strong hand to those engulfed by an abyss, *pray for us.*

You who countless nuns look to as their mother, *pray for us.*

You who are the helping friend of Poitiers, *pray for us.*

You who are concerned about the good of your people, *pray for us.*

You whose tomb for 14 centuries

has been a place where misery converges with grace, *pray for us.*

You who rejoice in seeing Jesus face to face, *pray for us, St. Radegund, so that we are worthy of the promises of Christ.*

Let Us Pray

Lord, grant us always the help we expect from the intercession of St. Radegund, the incomparable nun Queen, so that we, with a happy heart, will feel the effects of your immense love. Through Jesus Christ our Lord. *Amen.*

"*King Dagobert offering his son Sigebert to St. Amand, who had been banished before by the king*" *by Jean De Vignay (1463). Courtesy Wikimedia Commons.*

St. Sigebert III, King of Austrasia & Confessor

(630-656 A.D.)

Feast Day: January 30 or February 1, 3

• *Also known as Sigibert, Siegebert, or Sigisbert.*

• *Son of King Dagobert I of France and Bagnetrude.*

• *His father converted at the birth of Sigebert & wanted his son raised in the faith. Seeking the infant's baptism by a holy man, the king recalled St. Amand, who he had banished for remonstrating about his previous dissolute life. Sigebert's education was entrusted to Blessed Pepin of Landen.*

• *The king declared Sigebert at age 3 the successor of Austrasia & gave him St. Cunibert, archbishop of Cologne, as a minister.*

• *Austrasia spanned areas of today's Germany, France, Luxembourg, Belgium & the Netherlands.*

• *Upon his father's death, Sigebert became king at age 8. At 10 years old, he led an army in an unsuccessful attempt to acquire Thuringia.*

• *Married Queen Chimnechild of Burgundy. Their son was St. Dagobert II, and granddaughters were St. Irmina & St. Adela.*

• *His life was devoted to prayer & good works. During his*

reign, he built numerous homes for the poor, hospitals & churches, founding 12 monasteries.

- He died at age 26. He is the patron saint of Nancy, France.

Prayer in Honor of St. Sigebert

(translated from French)

Lord God, you have passed the holy Sigebert from earthly kingship to the glory of the kingdom of Heaven, we ask you, through his merits and intercession, let us share the kingship of Jesus Christ your Son, the King of kings. *Amen.*

Communion Prayer for the Graces of St. Sigebert

(translated from French)

He was faithful to the commandments of God, the Lord strengthened the kingdom in his hands, and he had riches and honor in abundance.

O God, as you filled your holy Sigebert with help overcoming the temptations of this world, may we, by this sacrament we receive, follow his example to push away the attractions of this world and come to you with purity of heart. *Amen.*

Prayer to St. Sigebert

(translated from French)

His miracles made him famous, who can boast of being like him? During his life, he did wonders; and in death; he did miracles.

Almighty God, as King St. Sigebert, despising the riches of this world, strove to please only Christ the King, we pray you, through his intercession let us renounce vain things, and with a pure heart follow you the only true God. *Amen.*

"King St. Dagobert II" by Nicolas de Larmessin (1690). Courtesy Wikimedia Commons.

St. Dagobert II, King of Austrasia & Martyr

(652-679 A.D.)

Feast Day: November 7 & December 23

• *Son of Immichilde of Burgundy & King St. Sigebert II of the Merovingian dynasty.*

• *After his father's death, his guardian put his own son on the throne & sent 7-year-old Dagobert into exile to England and Ireland.*

• *He stayed there and married Mechtilde, an English princess. They had several children. Two of his daughters became abbesses: St. Irmina, who founded a*

Benedictine convent in Trier, & St. Adela, a widow.

• *Later his cousin became king. After that king's murder, Dagobert II returned to Metz & gained the throne 18 years after his father's death the help of St. Wilfred, bishop of York.*

• **Living mainly in Alsace, King Dagobert II was a generous king devoted to his faith & his subjects. He built churches & founded a monastery in Strasbourg.**

• **He was murdered in a forest by assassins sent by political opponents.**

Prayer to St. Dagobert

(translated from French)

O God, who has given your people the saintly King Dagobert, we ask you, through the prayers of this great intercessor, deliver us from our enemies everywhere and grant us the joy that you render in quiet prosperity.

Grant us, we ask you Almighty God, through the glorious intercession of blessed King Dagobert, your martyr, that we also share your heavenly kingdom, and free us from the evil holds of sin here in exile. Through Christ our Lord. *Amen.*

"Mass being celebrated for the coronation of Claude of France" in Le Sacre de Claude de France (circa 1517). Courtesy The British Library.

Prayer to St. Dagobert during Mass

(translated from French)

Lord, we ask you, sanctify our offerings, that through the intercession of blessed King Dagobert, your martyr, we may become heirs of your heavenly kingdom. *Amen.*

"King Henry & St. Matilda" (center) by Konrad Astfalck (1896). Courtesy Wikimedia Commons.

St. Matilda, Queen of Germany

(895-968 A.D.)

Feast Day: March 14

• *Also known as Mathildis, Maude, Mechtild & Methildis. She was born in northern Germany.*

• *Daughter of Count Dietrich, prince of Saxony, & Reinhilda. She was raised in a monastery.*

• *Married King Henry I, the Fowler, after his first marriage was declared invalid. She became stepmother to Otto I, Holy Roman Emperor, St. Bruno & their siblings.*

• *Her husband gained the throne from 918 to his death in 936.*

- *She gave generously to the poor & was accused by her sons later in life for impoverishing the treasury by donating so much to charity. She built monasteries in Engern, Nordhausen, Poehlden & Quedlinburg.*

- *She lived a devout life, renounced her possessions & died at a convent in Quedlinburg.*

Prayer to St. Matilda

(translated from early 1700s French prayer)

Lord, grant us the grace of humility and patience through the intercession of St. Matilda your servant, so that while we honor her merits, we may feel the effects of her assistance. Through our Lord Jesus Christ your Son. *Amen.*

Prayer in Honor of St. Matilda

(translated from early 1800s French prayer)

O God, the only hope of the souls of saints, who, exiled from you on earth, strongly felt the pain of this separation. We ask that by praying night and day, we may, according to the example of St. Matilda, deserve to participate with her in heavenly consolations. Through our Lord Jesus Christ your Son. So be it. *Amen.*

"St. Adelaide". Courtesy Wikimedia Commons.

St. Adelaide, Holy Roman Empress, Queen of Italy & Germany

(931-999 A.D.)

Feast Day: December 16

• *Born in what is now Switzerland, she is also known as St. Adelaide of Italy. Also called Adelhaid, Adelaida & Alice.*

• *Daughter of Rudolf II of Burgundy & Bertha of Swabia.*

• *At 15 she was married for political reasons to the Lothair II, King of Italy, who was poisoned by a rival. She was imprisoned & freed by a priest. She escaped with the help of Otto the Great.*

• *A year later, she became the 2nd wife to Otto the Great, Holy Roman Emperor. Upon the death of her son Otto II, she was appointed co-regent for her grandson Otto III until he came of age.*

• **She was known for governing with wisdom & taking no revenge on enemies in court intrigues. She is described as conducting her court like religious houses and being a peacemaker of Europe.**

• **Building many monasteries & churches, she was also interested in the conversion of Slavs. She retired to a Benedictine Abby in Selz, France, and was canonized in 1097 by Pope Urban II.**

• **Patron of abuse victims, exiles, prisoners & princesses.**

Feast Day Prayer for St. Adelaide

(translated from early 1800s French prayer)

O God, grant that as we celebrate the happy day of St. Adelaide, we are instructed by her example. Make us, through her merits, always obedient to the commandments of the Lord. Grant us the daily intercessions of blessed Adelaide that we may be able to become holy and without blemish.

With all kinds of blessings, O Lord, bless us and protect us, your children who are flesh and blood, and help us with the prayers and services of blessed Adelaide, who was constantly filled with the Holy Spirit.

Grant, we beseech you, Almighty God, that we, who under the weight of our sins, may gain your blessing through intercession of Blessed Adelaide. Through Christ our Lord.

Amen.

"King Henry II" by Richard Wagner (1903).
Courtesy Wikimedia Commons.

St. Henry II, German King & Holy Roman Emperor

(972-1024 A.D.)

Feast Day: July 13 or 15

• *An oblate of the Benedictine Order, he is main patron of the oblates.*

• *Son of Duke Henry II, duke of Bavaria & Gisella of Burgundy. He was closely related to the kings of Germany and France.*

• *Married St. Cunigunde of Luxembourg. They both took vows of chastity and had no children.*

• *He was made emperor when his cousin died. During his*

reign, he made large donations of imperial land to monasteries, supported churches & promoted monastic reforms.

* *He built the Cathedral of Bamberg. Pope Eugene II canonized him in 1146.*

* *He had a special devotion to the Blessed Virgin Mary & saw a vision in which she sent an angel to him with a book to kiss during Mass. The angel said "Accept this sign of God's love for your chastity & justice" and then touched his leg. From that time, Henry became lame.*

* *Patron of the childless, of dukes, those rejected by religious orders, the handicapped & of Basel, Switzerland.*

Prayer for the Virtues of St. Henry

(translated from early 1700s French prayer)

Giving us the grace of baptism, Lord, you have the honor to make us kings or penitents for you are our God. Grant us by the prayers of St. Henry, who worked throughout his life for you, that we may control our passions by subjecting them to your sacred laws. That by sacrifice, we may continuously perform penance and the practice of all the virtues, so that we may number among your children in eternity. *Amen.*

"*Henry gives lecture on ethics*" *by Laurentius de Voltolina (circa 1450). Courtesy Wikimedia Commons.*

On the Feast Day of St. Henry

(translated from early 1700s German prayer)

O God, who on this day took blessed Henry your confessor from his earthly throne to an eternal kingdom, we humbly ask to be assisted by your grace, as St. Henry was, to stand against all the temptations of the world, so we may follow his example in withstanding all the flatteries of this world, and serve you with clean hearts. Through Christ our Lord. *Amen.*

Benedictine Prayer for the Strength of St. Henry

This man, despising the world and triumphing over earthly things, has laid up treasure in heaven by word and deed.

• *The Lord led the just one through right ways.*

• *And showed him the kingdom of God.*

O God, who removed blessed Henry your Confessor from the government of an earthly empire and raised him to the kingdom of Heaven.

We humbly ask you that, just as by the fullness of your grace you gave him strength to overcome the enticements of this life, so you would enable us, through his example, to shun the blandishments of this world and come to you with clean hearts. Through Christ our Lord. *Amen.*

"Genealogy of St. Henry II" (upper left) by Hartmann Schedel (1440-1514). Courtesy Wikimedia Commons.

For St. Henry's Intercession

O God, whose abundant grace prepared St. Henry to be raised by you in a wonderful way from the cares of earthly rule to heavenly realms, grant, we pray, through his intercession, that amid the uncertainties of this world we may hasten towards you with minds made pure. Through our Lord Jesus Christ, your Son, who lives and reigns with you in the unity of the Holy Spirit, one God, forever and ever. *Amen.*

*"Coronation of the Virgin of Mercy in Bavaria"
by Martin von Feuerstein (1889). Courtesy
Wikimedia Commons.*

Germany's Patron Saints

Prayer before the Mariensäule

Holy Mother of the Lord! Our ancestors, at a time of trouble, set up your statue in the very heart of Munich, and entrusted the city and country to your care. They wanted to meet you again and again along the paths of their daily life, and to learn from you the right way to live, to find God and to live in harmony. They gave you a crown and a scepter, which at that time were symbols of dominion over the country, because they knew that power and dominion would then be in good hands, in the hands of a Mother.

At the decisive hour in your own life, you said: "Here I am, the servant of the Lord". You lived your whole life as service. And you continue to do so throughout history.

At Cana, you silently and discreetly interceded for the spouses, and so you continue to do. You take upon yourself people's needs and concerns, and you bring them before the Lord, before your Son. Your power is goodness. Your power is service.

Teach us, great and small alike, to carry out our responsibilities in the same way. Help us to find the strength to offer reconciliation and forgiveness.

Help us to become patient and humble, but also free and courageous, just as you were at the hour of the Cross. In your arms you hold Jesus, the Child who blesses, the Child who is also the Lord of the world. By holding the Child who blesses, you have yourself become a blessing. Bless this country! Show us Jesus, the blessed fruit of your womb! Pray for us sinners, now and at the hour of our death. Amen.

(Pope Benedict XVI, 2006)

"St. Boniface" by Alfred Rethel (1832). Courtesy Wikimedia Commons.

Litany of Saint Boniface, Patron of Germany

Lord have mercy.

Lord have mercy.

Christ have mercy.

Christ have mercy.

Lord, have mercy.

Lord, have mercy.

Christ, hear us.

Christ graciously hear us.

God, the Father of Heaven, *have mercy on us.*

God, the Son, Redeemer of the world, *have mercy on us.*

God, the Holy Ghost, *have mercy on us.*

Holy Trinity, one God, *have mercy on us.*

Holy Mary, *pray for us.*

Holy Mother of God, *pray for us.*

Holy Virgin of virgins, *pray for us.*

Queen of the apostles, *pray for us.*

St. Boniface, *pray for us.*

Apostle of Germany, *pray for us.*

Worthy successor of the apostles, *pray for us.*

Worthy disciple of St. Benedict, *pray for us.*

Ornament of the Catholic Church, *pray for us.*

You a light, shining for the conversion of unbelieving nations, *pray for us.*

You a light, shining like the sun, *pray for us.*

You a great benefactor of many nations, *pray for us.*

You a zealous preacher of the Gospel, *pray for us.*

You an unwearied laborer in the vineyard of the Lord, *pray for us.*

You the founder of the Catholic Church in Germany, *pray for us.*

St. Boniface, our father, *pray for us.*

St. Boniface, teacher of truth and virtue, *pray for us.*

St. Boniface, eradicator of heathenism, *pray for us.*

St. Boniface, destroyer of heresy, *pray for us.*

St. Boniface, great bishop and model of missionaries, *pray for us.*

St. Boniface, protector of missions, *pray for us.*

St. Boniface, founder of many monasteries, *pray for us.*

St. Boniface, powerful advocate with God, *pray for us.*

St. Boniface, who worked many miracles, *pray for us.*

St. Boniface, great martyr of faith, *pray for us.*

That God may preserve and confirm us in our holy Catholic religion, *pray for us.*

That God may grant us grace to walk piously and faithfully before him, *pray for us.*

That God may convert the enemies of his Church, *pray for us.*

That God may grant the grace of true faith to all unbelievers, *pray for us.*

That God may give us that spirit with which you did serve him, *pray for us.*

That God may restore the faith to the whole of Germany, *pray for us.*

That God may raise up zealous missionaries to convert all unbelievers and heretics, *pray for us.*

That the Holy Spirit may enlighten all missionaries, *pray for us.*

Lamb of God, who takes away the sins of the world, *spare us, O Lord.*

Lamb of God, who takes away the sins of the world, *graciously hear us, O Lord.*

Lamb of God, who takes away the sins of the world, *have mercy on us.*

Christ hear us.

Christ graciously hear us.

Lord have mercy.

Christ have mercy.

Lord have mercy.

Let Us Pray

Merciful God, who showed compassion to so many unbelieving nations, through your faithful servant St. Boniface: we humbly pray you to revive and preserve that faith which he preached in your Holy Name, that we may receive your revelations with a faithful heart, and so conduct our lives as to gain the Heavenly Kingdom. Through Jesus Christ our Lord.

Preserve and increase, we ask you, O God, the faith of your children, and lead back to the true fold all those who have been separated or have separated themselves from it. Through Christ our Lord. *Amen.*

"St. Cunigunde" by Meister von Messkirch (circa 1535-1540). Courtesy Wikimedia Commons.

Chapter 5: Luxembourg

Saintly Luxembourg Empress

*"Angels in Adoration" by Benozzo Gozzoli
(1420-1497). Courtesy Wikimedia Commons.*

Nobility of the soul is preferable
to that of birth.

—*St. Ambrose (340–397 A.D.), Doctor
of the Catholic Church*

"Holy Roman Emperor Henry II and his wife Cunigunde" (circa 1500s). Courtesy Wikimedia Commons.

St. Cunigunde, Holy Roman Empress

(970-1040 A.D.)

Feast Day: March 3

• *Also known as Cunegund, Cunegonde or Kinga of Luxembourg.*

• *Patron of Luxembourg & Lithuania*

• *Descendant of Charlemagne.*

• *Daughter of Siegfried I of Luxembourg and Hedwig of Nordgau.*

• *Married Henry II, who was made emperor and canonized by the same Pope in 1146 as St. Henry.*

• *Prior marrying, she made a vow of virginity, which she continued with her husband's consent. The couple lived a devout life and gave significantly to the poor.*

• *Accused of adultery, she proved her virtue by walking over hot coals.*

• *She founded a Benedictine monastery in Germany to fulfill a promise upon recovering from an illness. After her husband died in 1024, she put on a nun's habit a year later and dedicated her life to serving God.*

St. Cunigunde
Feast Day Prayer

(translated from 1800s French prayer)

Graciously hear us, O God, who are our salvation, so that as we applaud the feast day of the happy St. Cunigunde, we may feel a stronger devotion to you. We ask this through Jesus Christ our Savior. So be it. Amen

*"St. Cunigunde walking over hot coals" by
unknown. Courtesy Wikimedia Commons.*

Prayer on the Feast Day of St. Cunigunde

(translated from early 1700s German prayer)

Lend us your ear, O God our Savior, so that as we celebrate with joy the solemnity of the blessed Cunigunde your virgin, so we my increase our love of holiness. We ask this through Jesus Christ our Lord. *Amen.*

*"St. Henry and St. Cunigunde" (circa 1400s).
Courtesy Wikimedia Commons.*

Prayer to St. Henry & St. Cunigunde

(translated from German)

Almighty God, you entrusted earthly power to the holy Emperor Henry and his wife, Cunigunde. For their work you rewarded them with the eternal glory.

Also give us the grace to that we fulfill our role in this world and become heirs of your kingdom be. We ask this through Jesus Christ. *Amen.*

"St. Willibrord" by Cornelis Bloemaert (circa 1630). Courtesy Wikimedia Commons.

Luxembourg's Patron Saints

For Luxembourg in Union with the Offering of Mass

Eternal Father, through the Immaculate Heart of Mary, I wish to unite myself with Jesus, now offering his precious blood in Luxembourg in the Holy Sacrifice of the Mass, for the holy church, for the conversion of sinners, the souls in Purgatory and the special grace I now ask (mention your request). Amen.

*"The Angel" by Carl Timoleon von Neff
(1804-1887). Courtesy Wikimedia Commons.*

To Jesus for Luxembourg

(translated from French)

O Christ, our Lord, beloved Son of the Father, our friend, and master who loves life and doesn't forget any creature.

Look upon the Church in Luxembourg, and send it the energizing breath and the fire of your spirit. Mark it with the seal of the Holy Spirit, remind the baptized that they are members of your body so they may live in their hearts by faith, be founded in love, and open up in them the praise of your glory.

O Christ, Lord, power and wisdom of God, you bring everything to fulfillment because the power of your love surpasses all understanding. You can give us more than we know to ask.

Give to your people the spirit of wisdom, open their hearts to contain your word and to respect the life of the family and society, work and leisure, childhood and youth, adulthood and old age.

O Christ, the wisdom of God, reflection shining of his glory and expression of his being, you move the universe with the power of your Word. Teach people the true meaning of the things of this world and the love of the eternal goods, so that they know how to use your gifts in discerning between good and evil.

Give them love in family relationships, justice in social relations, truth in communications, and reconciliation in conflict.

Help the people of Luxembourg to take the time, as did their fathers and all their brothers, to arm themselves against the forces of evil and live as children of light.

O Christ, Son of God, you took the form of a slave, and became similar to men until the death of the cross. Firstborn from the dead, risen Christ, by you it pleased the Father to reconcile all beings.

By our baptism in your death and your resurrection, you give us new life. By the Virgin Mary, your mother, and through her Immaculate Heart, we pray: help us to discover the treasures of wisdom hidden in you. With Mary, we want to retain them and reflect them in our hearts. With Mary, as she was amid the disciples, enable us to be faithful witnesses, in faith and love. *Amen.*

(Pope John Paul II, 1981)

"*Coming of St. Willibrord to the Netherlands*"
*by unknown (1903). Courtesy Wikimedia
Commons.*

Litany to St. Willibrord, Patron of Luxembourg

Lord have mercy,

Christ have mercy.

Christ hear our prayer.

Christ hear our prayer.

God the Father in Heaven, *have mercy on us.*

God the Son, Redeemer of the world, *have mercy on us.*

God the Holy Spirit, *have mercy on us.*

God the Holy Trinity, *have mercy on us.*

Blessed Mary, *pray for us.*

Blessed Mother of God, *pray for us.*

Blessed Virgin of all virgins, *pray for us.*

St. Willibrord, *pray for us.*

St. Willibrord, guiding light of the church, *pray for us.*

St. Willibrord, bright-shining star of our country, *pray for us.*

St. Willibrord, missionary to our homeland, *pray for us.*

St. Willibrord, special protector of this our land, *pray for us.*

St. Willibrord, first apostle of the Netherlands, *pray for us.*

St. Willibrord, founder of monasteries and churches, *pray for us.*

St. Willibrord, promoter of progress and knowledge, *pray for us.*

St. Willibrord, teacher of truth, *pray for us.*

St. Willibrord, passionate interpreter of the teaching of Christ, *pray for us.*

St. Willibrord, ceaseless proclaimer of the Holy Gospel, pray for us.

St. Willibrord, teacher of true faith, *pray for us.*

St. Willibrord, founder of peace and justice, *pray for us.*

St. Willibrord, model of hope and reconciliation, *pray for us.*

St. Willibrord, conqueror of injustice and discord, *pray for us.*

St. Willibrord, architect of community and unity, *pray for us.*

St. Willibrord, destroyer of idols, *pray for us.*

St. Willibrord, patron saint of children, *pray for us.*

St. Willibrord, gentle guide of the lost, *pray for us.*

St. Willibrord, support of the homeless, *pray for us.*

St. Willibrord, friend of the persecuted, *pray for us.*

St. Willibrord, light of the blind, *pray for us.*

St. Willibrord, refuge for the sick, *pray for us.*

St. Willibrord, gentle father of the poor, *pray for us.*

St. Willibrord, comforter of the afflicted and sorrowful, *pray for us.*

St. Willibrord, helper to the suffering, *pray for us.*

St. Willibrord, true voice of God, *pray for us.*

St. Willibrord, humble servant of Jesus Christ, *pray for us.*

St. Willibrord, mighty advocate in Heaven, *pray for us.*

St. Willibrord, miraculous healer, *pray for us.*

St. Willibrord, true witness and confessor of Christ, *pray for us.*

St. Willibrord, savior of those who doubt their faith, *pray for us.*

St. Willibrord, supporter of caretakers and educators, *pray for us.*

St. Willibrord, hope of those who pray, *pray for us.*

St. Willibrord, model of patience and gentleness, *pray for us.*

St. Willibrord, example of active love, *pray for us.*

St. Willibrord, master of joy and life, *pray for us.*

St. Willibrord, disciple of Christ, *pray for us.*

Lamb of God you take away the sins of the world.

Lord have mercy on us.

Lamb of God you take away the sins of the world.

Lord hear our prayer.

Lamb of God you take away the sins of the world.

Lord have mercy on us. *Amen.*

*"King & Queen with a nun and attendants" from
the Stowe Breviary (circa 1300s). Courtesy The
British Library.*

Chapter 6:
Switzerland

Swiss Kings

The brightest ornaments in the crown of the blessed in Heaven are the sufferings which they have borne patiently on earth.

*—St. Alphonsus de Liguori (1696– 1787),
Doctor Most Zealous of the Catholic Church*

"King Zwentibold with a bishop and the queen"
(circa 1300s). Courtesy Wikimedia Commons.

St. Zwentibold, King of Lotharingia, Martyr (Lorraine)

(871-900 A.D.)

Feast Day: August 13

• *Also known as Zwenteboldus, Zuentipoldus, Zuentibold & Swatopluk.*

• *The kingdom of Lotharingia was part of today's Switzerland.*

• *Illegitimate son of Arnulf of Carinthia, King of East Francia & disputed king of Italy & the Holy Roman Empire.*

• *His grandfather was Carloman, King of Bavaria & King of Italy.*

• *Married Oda, daughter of Otto I, Duke of Saxony.*

- *Succeeded his father in 895 as king.*

- *Promoted Christianity, viewed the prosperity of his people as important, and built churches & convents. Gave tithes from an abbey to the poor and travelers.*

- *His assistance to the community caused ill will from fellow nobles.*

- *With backing from his father & archbishops, he tried to integrate his kingdom with the East Frankish realm.*

- *A dispute with nobles arose after his father's death in 899 A.D.*

- *He died in battle in the Netherlands in a confrontation with rebels in a battle led by a duke of Lorraine.*

- *He was buried in a former Benedictine abbey (Susteren) in what is now St. Amelberga*

Basilica where his daughters were nuns.

Prayer to St. Zwentibold and to the Saints & Angels

(translated from 1800s French prayer)

All you holy saints of God, particularly you, St. Zwentibold, and all you holy angels of God, especially you whom God has appointed to be my guardian, intercede for me, and defend me from all danger. Amen.

"King Zwentibold looking at his court" (circa 1300s). Courtesy Wikimedia Commons.

Prayer to
St. Zwentibold

O Blessed St. Zwentibold, glorious citizen of Heaven, as I give my most humble thanks to God for all the good he has done you.

I ask you to remember me in your prayers, and to obtain for me the entire pardon of my sins, the amendment of my life, and the imitation of your good spirit and holy graces, that I may be reconciled to my Savior and always please him.

But especially I recommend to you the hour of my death that, by your holy intercession, my soul may depart from this world in the grace of God, and may immediately come to everlasting life. *Amen.*

"St. Sigismund" by Lorenzo Lotto (1508).
Courtesy Wikimedia Commons.

St. Sigismund, King of Burgundy & Martyr

(died 526 A.D.)

Feast Day: August 13

• *Son of Gondebald, the Arian king of Burgundy. Succeeded his father to French throne in 516.*

• *The kingdom of Burgundy was part of today's Switzerland.*

• *Married Ostrogotha, daughter of a king. When she died, he married a woman of inferior status, who despised his older son.*

• *Converted by St. Avitus, bishop of Vienna. He founded a monastery to St. Maurice in present day Switzerland. He created favorable policies to the* church & was generous with his subjects.

• *Although devout after his conversion and charitable on the throne, he was tricked & in a fit of rage ordered the killing of his son, who had been falsely accused by the stepmother queen of conspiring to kill the king. Discovering the truth & full of remorse, he left to a monastery where he did penance and prayed to be punished in this life to avoid divine vengeance in the next.*

• *Soon afterwards, to avenge his grandfather's killing by Gondebald, the king of the Franks declared war on Sigismund, who was living as a hermit monk after the murder of his son.*

• *Sigismund was captured in monk's attire. Despite pleadings by St. Avitus, Sigismund, his wife*

& children were drowned in a well. Their bodies lay for 3 years until burial. Miracles at the well were attributed to the intercession of Sigismund, declared a martyr.

• *In 515 A.D., St. Sigismund founded in Valais, Switzerland, the Abbey of Saint-Maurice for 5 groups of monks to pray a special liturgy for the perpetual praise of God in memory of martyrs of the Theban Legion*

• *The abbey, still in existence, features a Shrine of the Children of Saint Sigismund (from the 12th to 13th centuries) built for the relics of his sons Giscald and Gondebald II.*

• *In the 14th century, his relics were transferred to Prague. He is a patron of penitents & the Czech Republic.*

Prayer on the Feast of St. Sigismund

(translated from German)

Holy God, you are the king, who chose Sigismund to lead his people to the true faith. You graciously accepted his penance for past wrongs.

Grant us the grace, through his intercession, so that we also may overcome evil and find mercy with you. We ask this through Jesus Christ. *Amen.*

Prayer for those Sick with a Fever through St. Sigismund

(from the 11th Century)

Almighty and everlasting God, who by your holy apostles and martyrs bestowed diverse gifts of healing, grant we ask you, to raise up to health by your medicine your servant (name), who is grievously vexed by fever, and mercifully restore (him/her) whole through the intercession of your servant Sigismund, king and martyr.

We offer you this prayer, O Lord, in the name of Sigismund, your chosen king and martyr, that you would end the burning fever of this sick person, and ever defend (him/ her) by your aid.

Almighty and everlasting God, who grants to those who minister before you the fulfillment of all those things that they rightly ask, mercifully receive our prayers offered on behalf of your servant (name) in honor of St. Sigismund, your king and martyr.

Grant what we ask with a devout mind for this person so that we may speedily obtain it by your favor. Through Christ our Lord. *Amen.*

"St. Gallen preaching" by unknown. Courtesy Wikimedia Commons.

Switzerland's Patron Saints

Prayer to St. Gallen, Patron of Switzerland

O God, who was pleased to provide for your Church, in example of the good Shepherd, St. Gallen. Mercifully grant that through his intercession we may be found worthy to be placed in your pasture forever. Through Christ our Lord. Amen.

Prayer to
Our Lady of Vorbourg

(translated from early 1700s French prayer)

O glorious and very kind mother of my Savior, my powerful Queen of the angels and charitable counsel for fishermen who have chosen the Holy Chapel of the Vorbourg as a place where graces are distributed after it was consecrated by Pope St. Leo IX.

Despite my unworthiness, I implore you through you my God's mercy for your assistance and acknowledge the obvious miracles through your intercession, which arise from the Holy Chapel of Vorbourg, which so many people have chosen as a shelter amid all their needs.

The wonderful graces and blessings being spread by you daily are powerful reasons to invite me to prostrate myself at your feet to ask for graces you know are necessary for me.

O charitable mother, watch over your unworthy servant with your merciful eyes, which cannot bear to look upon the unhappy without providing relief.

Extend your protection, as in Vorbourg, over our parish and our diocese against the insults of our enemies, internal and external, visible and invisible.

Never withdraw your powerful assistance from me or any of those dear to me.

Keep away from us anything that could harm us in body and soul. Dispense a few drops of your inexhaustible graces and blessings on us.

Defend us especially at the terrible time of death so that dying quietly we be an example of your mercy to praise and bless forever with you, the Father, the Son, and the Holy Spirit. *Amen.*

Marie Noël

Prayer for the Papal Swiss Guards

(translated from German & provided by the Swiss Guard)

Almighty eternal God, for 505 years the Swiss Guards have stood in service of the successors of St. Peter, we thank you for all of these years which you, in your providence have given to us, and we ask you to continue to preserve the Guards in their loyalty to the Holy Father and to the Catholic Church.

Hold your protective hand over our Pope and bestow on him the gifts of the Holy Ghost.

We pray to you for all the relatives of the Swiss Guards: protect and strengthen the weak, enlighten the doubting, comfort the afflicted, and lead those astray back to the way.

Be always with us with your assisting grace, which bears the burdens of others.

Give eternal life to our departed and gather them in your splendor.

Bless their homeland Switzerland and preserve your people in faithfulness to you. *Amen.*

"*A Swiss Guard protects a conclave with the Pope*" *by unknown (1578). Courtesy Wikimedia Commons.*

Another Prayer for the Pontifical Swiss Guards

(by Pope Benedict XVI in May 2006 on the 500th anniversary when the first 150 Swiss Guards arrived in Rome, at the request of Pope Julius II - marking the start of their Papal service)

May the Virgin Mary and their patrons, St. Martin, St. Sebastian and St. Nicholas of Flüe, help the Swiss Guards to carry out their daily tasks with generous dedication, ever enlivened by a spirit of faith and love for the Church. *Amen.*

"A priest visits St. Nicholas of Flüe" by Diebold Schilling the Younger (1513). Courtesy Wikimedia Commons.

Litany of St. Nicholas of Flüe, Patron of Switzerland

(translated from German)

Lord have mercy on us.

Christ have mercy on us.

Lord have mercy on us.

Christ hear us.

Christ hear us.

God the Father of Heaven, *have mercy on us.*

God the Son, Redeemer of the world, *have mercy on us.*

God the Holy Spirit, *have mercy on us.*

Holy Trinity, one God, *have mercy on us.*

Holy Mary, *pray for us.*

Holy Brother Klaus, *pray for us.*

St. Nicholas, example for brave parents, *pray for us.*

St. Nicholas, who showed filial piety, *pray for us.*

St. Nicholas, mirror for young people, *pray for us.*

St. Nicholas, model of Christian men, *pray for us.*

St. Nicholas, faithful husband, *pray for us.*

St. Nicholas, conscientious father, *pray for us.*

St. Nicholas, who took education seriously, *pray for us.*

St. Nicholas, good farmer, *pray for us.*

St. Nicholas, model of frugality and generosity, *pray for us.*

St. Nicholas, lover of simplicity and

humility, *pray for us.*

St. Nicholas, noble soldier, *pray for us.*

St. Nicholas, protector of the weak, *pray for us.*

St. Nicholas, friend of the poor, *pray for us.*

St. Nicholas, pious pilgrim, *pray for us.*

St. Nicholas, benefactor of poor churches, *pray for us.*

St. Nicholas, zealous lay apostle, *pray for us.*

St. Nicholas, enemy of human fear, *pray for us.*

St. Nicholas, just judge, *pray for us.*

St. Nicholas, clever statesman, *pray for us.*

St. Nicholas, who shunned earthly possessions, pleasures & honors, *pray for us.*

St. Nicholas, holy hermit, *pray for us.*

St. Nicholas, man of destiny, *pray for us.*

St. Nicholas, strict penitent, *pray for us.*

St. Nicholas, master of prayer, *pray for us.*

St. Nicholas, model of the interior life, *pray for us.*

St. Nicholas, victor over the temptations of Satan, *pray for us.*

St. Nicholas, hero of self-control, *pray for us.*

St. Nicholas, tower of the spirit, *pray for us.*

St. Nicholas, bright star and good example, *pray for us.*

St. Nicholas, great admirer of the Holy Trinity, *pray for us.*

St. Nicholas, intimate observer of

Christ's suffering, *pray for us.*

St. Nicholas, appreciator of Eucharistic wonders, *pray for us.*

St. Nicholas, living proof of the power of Holy Communion, *pray for us.*

St. Nicholas, avid attendant at Mass, *pray for us.*

St. Nicholas, silent prayer before the tabernacle, *pray for us.*

St. Nicholas, delicate admirer of the Virgin Mother of God, *pray for us.*

St. Nicholas, helper of the poor, *pray for us.*

St. Nicholas, who had knowledge of the heart and of things to come, *pray for us.*

St. Nicholas, fatherly example for sinners, *pray for us.*

St. Nicholas, consoler of the unfortunate, *pray for us.*

St. Nicholas, wise counselor, *pray for*

us.

St. Nicholas, friend of priests, *pray for us.*

St. Nicholas, teacher of the people, *pray for us.*

St. Nicholas, peacemaker sent by God, *pray for us.*

St. Nicholas, savior of Switzerland, *pray for us.*

St. Nicholas, champion of the Catholic faith, *pray for us.*

St. Nicholas, supporter of religious unity, *pray for us.*

St. Nicholas, wonder-working helper, *pray for us.*

St. Nicholas, intercessor before the throne of God, *pray for us.*

St. Nicholas, saint of Switzerland, *pray for us.*

O Lamb of God who takes away the sins of the world. *Spare a us, O Lord.*

O Lamb of God who takes away the sins of the world. *Hear us, O Lord.*

O Lamb of God who takes away the sins of the world. *Have mercy on us, O Lord.*

Pray for us, O holy Brother Klaus.

That we may be made worthy of the promises of Christ.

Let Us Pray

O God, who fed the holy hermit Nicholas with the wonderful food of angels and bestowed on him abundant heavenly gifts, grant us, we ask you, through his intercession, that we may partake of the Body and Blood of the Lord worthily on earth, and be with you in Heaven. Through Christ our Lord. *Amen.*

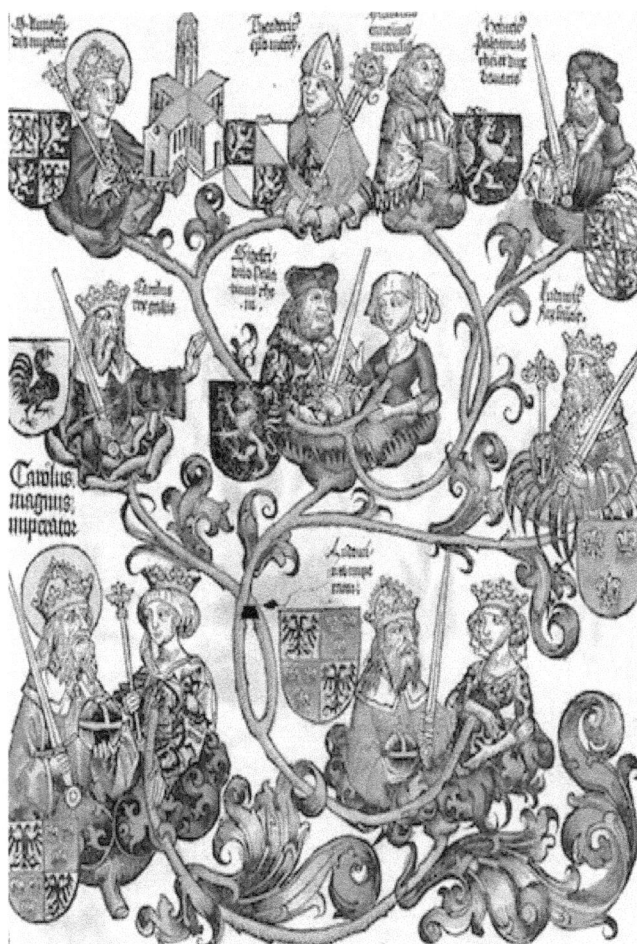

*"Family tree of Empress Cunigunde" (top left)
from the Nuremberg Chronicle (1493). Courtesy
Wikimedia Commons.*

Chapter 7:

Royal Litanies

Litanies to the Saints

*"Queen and monk" by unknown from French
illuminated manuscript (circa 1400s). Courtesy
The British Library.*

A precious crown is reserved in heaven for those who perform all their actions with all the diligence of which they are capable; for it is not sufficient to do our part well; it must be done more than well.

—*St. Ignatius of Loyola (1491–1556)*

Holy Catholic Queens & Empresses

O God, who by the grace of your benediction did raise up Holy Catholic Queens and Empresses to heaven, sanctify your people, we ask you, with a new benediction of your grace, and through their prayers and merits, defend us by your power from all the evils that threaten us. Through Christ our Lord. Amen.

Litany of the Holy Kings

(translated from early 1800s French prayer)

Jesus of Nazareth, *have mercy on us.*

Holy David the king, *pray for us.*

All you Holy Magi, *pray for us.*

St. Louis, king of France, *pray for us.*

St. Gontran, king of Orleans and Burgundy, and confessor, *pray for us.*

St. Sigismund, king of Burgundy and martyr, *pray for us.*

St. Sigebert, king of Austrasia, *pray for us.*

*"St. Sigismond" by anonymous. Courtesy The
British Library.*

St. Edwin, king of Northumbria, *pray for us.*

St. Edmond, king of East Anglia and martyr, *pray for us.*

St. Ethelbert, king of Kent, *pray for us.*

St. Edward, king of England and confessor, *pray for us.*

St. Elesbaan, king of Ethiopia and confessor, *pray for us.*

St. Edward, king of England and martyr, *pray for us.*

St. Eric, king of Sweden and martyr, *pray for us.*

St. Stephen, king of Hungary, *pray for us.*

St. Ferdinand, king of Castile & Leon, *pray for us.*

St. Henry, king of Germany & Holy Roman Empire, *pray for us.*

St. Ladislaus, king of Hungary, *pray for us.*

St. Richard, king of England and confessor, *pray for us.*

St. Sebbe, king of Essex, *pray for us.*

St. Canute, king of Denmark, *pray for us.*

Lamb of God who takes away the sins of the world, *pardon us.*

Lamb of God who takes away the sins of the world, *hear us.*

Lamb of God who takes away the sins of the world, *have pity on us.*

Lord, save us & all the kings and queens.

And hear us when we call on you. Amen.

Litany to Military Saints & Holy Royal Rulers

(translated from early 1800s French prayer)

Lord have mercy.

Christ have mercy.

Lord have mercy.

Christ hear us.

Christ graciously hear us.

God the Father of Heaven, *have mercy on us.*

God the Son, Redeemer of the world, *have mercy on us.*

God the Holy Spirit, *have mercy on us.*

Holy Trinity, one God, *have mercy on us.*

O Lord, God of hosts, God of the warriors of our ancestors, *have mercy on us.*

King of kings, Lord of lords, *have mercy on us.*

He who takes away kingdoms & establishes empires, *have mercy on us.*

He whose reign is eternal, *have mercy on us.*

He for whom belongs all grandeur, glory & victory, *have mercy on us.*

In whose hands lie our destinies, *have mercy on us.*

O Mary, Queen of the heavens & protector of the French, *pray for us.*

St. Michael the prince of the heavenly host & you blessed angels who have triumphed over the enemies of the Most High, *pray for us.*

All you holy patriarchs & holy warriors of the old covenant, who in the fighting have so often experienced the protection of God, *pray for us.*

Military saints of all ages who have followed the church of Jesus Christ, *pray for us.*

St. Valentine, *pray for us.*

St. Theodore, *pray for us.*

St. Milles, *pray for us.*

St. Eustace, *pray for us.*

St. George, *pray for us.*

St. Maurice, *pray for us.*

St. Ferreol, *pray for us.*

St. Philorome, *pray for us.*

St. Nicostratus, *pray for us.*

St. Sebastian, *pray for us.*

Sts. Exupere & Candide, *pray for us.*

St Adrian, *pray for us.*

Sts. Bonosus & Maximilian, *pray for us.*

St. Marcellus, *pray for us.*

St. Acacius, *pray for us.*

St. Hermione, *pray for us.*

St. Romain, *pray for us.*

Sts. Victor & Féciliane, *pray for us.*

St. Eleutherius, *pray for us.*

St. Eudoxi, *pray for us.*

St. Julian the Hospitaller, *pray for us.*

St. Theodore the younger, *pray for us.*

St. Callistratus, *pray for us.*

St. Cyrion, *pray for us.*

St. Severine, *pray for us.*

St. Leontius, *pray for us.*

St. Hermengild, king of the Visigoths,

pray for us.

St. Edmund, king of East Anglia, *pray for us.*

St. Canute, king of Denmark, *pray for us.*

St. Eric, king of Sweden, *pray for us.*

St. Wenceslas, king of the Czechs, *pray for us.*

All you holy kings & holy warriors who were martyred, *pray for us.*

St. Henry, king of Germany, *pray for us.*

St. Louis, king of France, *pray for us.*

St. Ferdinand, king of Leon and Castile, *pray for us.*

St. Stephen, king of Hungary, *pray for us.*

St. Ladislas, king of Hungary, *pray for us.*

St. Edward, king of England, *pray for us.*

"Coronation of St. Henry" by anonymous from
the Sacramentary of Henry II (circa 11th
century). Courtesy Wikimedia Commons.

St. Casimir, prince of Poland, *pray for us.*

St. Leopold, margrave of Austria, *pray for us.*

Holy emperors, kings & princes, *pray for us.*

St. Martin, *pray for us.*

St. Victricius, *pray for us.*

St. Arsacius, *pray for us.*

St. Pachomius, *pray for us.*

St. John Gualberto, *pray for us.*

St. Jerome Emiliani, *pray for us.*

St. John of God, *pray for us.*

St. Ignatius of Loyola, *pray for us.*

St. Camillus de Lellis, *pray for us.*

All you holy pontiffs, solitary saints & religious who have been soldiers, *pray for us.*

All you noble warriors who managed

to combine the service of the state with that of God, *pray for us.*

You who valiantly fought for your country & leaders, *pray for us.*

You who triumphed over your passions & your most formidable enemies, *pray for us.*

You who kept pure in the midst of promiscuity in camps & were blameless in your conversations, *pray for us.*

You who preferred the honors of heaven to the pleasures & riches of the earth, *pray for us.*

You who sacrificed and suffered to be crowned forever with heavenly glory & honor, *pray for us.*

For the saints who were soldiers that inspired love of your law & were the apex of heroism for Christian virtues, *O God of hosts, hear us.*

May we, by their example, worship

in spirit & truth and never be ashamed of our faith, *O God of hosts, hear us.*

That we may love you with all our heart, all our soul & all our strength, *O God of hosts, hear us.*

That we will observe with fidelity your Holy Commandments & be loyal to your Church, *O God of hosts, hear us.*

That we will sanctify all dedicated holy days, *O God of hosts, hear us.*

That we will never take your adorable name in vain, *O God of hosts, hear us.*

That we will never profane holiness by blasphemy, *O God of hosts, hear us.*

That we honor our spiritual and earthly leaders, *O God of hosts, hear us.*

That we may love our neighbors as ourselves for love of you, *O God of hosts, hear us.*

That we would behave towards others in the same way we would like others to act towards us, *O God of hosts, hear us.*

That we do not endanger the lives, reputation & property of our neighbors, *O God of hosts, hear us.*

That we abhor anger, slander, backbiting, lying & duplicity, *O God of hosts, hear us.*

That we do not defile our bodies by the depravity of avarice, drunkenness & uncleanness, *O God of hosts, hear us.*

That we always walk, act & suffer with you in the spirit of penance, *O God of hosts, hear us.*

That by your grace & our efforts we will conquer ourselves to live forever with you in your kingdom, *hear us, O God of hosts, hear us.*

Lamb of God who takes away the sins of the world, *graciously hear us, O Lord.*

Lamb of God who takes away the sins of the world, *spare us, O Lord.*

Lamb of God who takes away the sins of the world, *have mercy on us*

Christ hear us. *Christ graciously hear us.*

Pray for us all holy warriors of God, *that we may be made worthy of the promises of Christ.*

Let Us Pray

O God, through whose infinite wisdom and goodness we offer your the military saints as great models and powerful protectors, grant us, through their intercession, the obedience of faith, a firm hope, strength, compassion in your service, and the abundance of your eternal mercy. Through Christ our Lord. *Amen.*

"*Triumph of St. Hermengild, king of the Visigoths*" *by Francisco de Herrera II (1654). Courtesy Wikimedia Commons.*

Litany to Ancient Saints & Royals from the Early Church to the 6th Century

(translated from 1600s French prayer)

Lord have mercy on us.

Christ have mercy on us.

Lord have mercy on us.

Christ have mercy on us.

Christ hear us.

Father, Son and Holy Spirit, which are all one God, *have mercy on us.*

God the Son, Redeemer of the world, *have mercy on us.*

Holy Virgin Mary, Mother of God, *pray for us.*

All orders of blessed saints, *pray for us.*

St. Joseph, *pray for us.*

St. Tobias, *pray for us.*

St. Daniel, *pray for us.*

All you holy prophets and holy patriarchs, *pray for us.*

St. Bartholomew, *pray for us.*

St. Matthew, *pray for us.*

All you holy apostles and holy evangelists, *pray for us.*

St. Sigismund, king of Burgundy, who died in 526, *pray for us.*

Pope St. John I, *pray for us.*

St. Placidius, his sister St. Flavia & companions who were martyred in Sicily in 540, *pray for us.*

St. Hermengild, king of the Visigoths in Spain, who died in 584, *pray for us.*

All you holy martyrs, *pray for us.*

St. Eugene, confessor & bishop of

Carthage, who died in 505, *pray for us.*

St. Victor, confessor & bishop of Vita in Africa, who died in 507, *pray for us.*

St. Avitus, confessor & Archbishop of Vienna, who died in 525, *pray for us.*

St. Fulgentius, Bishop of Ruspe in Africa, who died in 533, *pray for us.*

St. Remigius, apostle of the Franks & Archbishop of Reims, who died in 533, *pray for us.*

St. Gregory, Bishop of Langres, who died in 541, *pray for us.*

St. Caesarius, Bishop of Arles & theologian, who died in 542, *pray for us.*

St. Innocent, Bishop of Le Mans, who died in 543, *pray for us.*

St. Medardus, Bishop of Noyon, who died in 545, *pray for us.*

St. Aulbinus, Bishop of Angers, who died in 550, *pray for us.*

St. Leobinus, hermit, abbot & Bishop of Chartres, who died in 556, *pray for us.*

St. John the Silent, Bishop of Colonia in Palestine, who died in 559, *pray for us.*

St. Samson, Bishop of Dol in Normandy, who died in 564, *pray for us.*

St. Nicetius, Bishop of Trier in Germany, who died in 565, *pray for us.*

St. Vedast, Bishop of Arras, who died in 570, *pray for us.*

St. Martin, Archbishop of Braga in Portugal, who died in 572, *pray for us.*

St. Eufronius, Bishop of Tours, who died in 573, *pray for us.*

St. Magloire, abbot of Dol in Brittany, who died in 575, *pray for us.*

St. Germain, Bishop of Paris, who died in 576, *pray for us.*

St. Domnole, Bishop of Le Mans, who died in 584, *pray for us.*

St. Sulpice, Bishop of Bourges, who died in 591, *pray for us.*

St. Gregory, Bishop of Tours, who died in 595, *pray for us.*

St. Leander, Bishop of Seville, who died in 596, *pray for us.*

All you holy bishops, *pray for us.*

St. Memin, abbot of Orleans, who died in 520, *pray for us.*

St. Severin, abbot of Paris, who died in 525, *pray for us.*

St. Avitus, abbot of Orleans, who died in 530, *pray for us.*

St. Theodosius, the Cernobiarch of Jerusalem, who died in 529, *pray for us.*

St. Sabas, Patriarch of the monks of Palestine, who died in 532, *pray for us.*

St. Calais, abbot of Anisola, who died in 541, *pray for us.*

"Glorification of St. Clotilde, Queen of France"
by unknown. Courtesy Wikimedia Commons.

St. Clodoald, priest of Paris, who died in 560, *pray for us.*

St. Equice, abbot of France, who died in 573, *pray for us.*

St. Maurus, abbot of Anjou, who died in 584, *pray for us.*

St. John Climacus, abbot of Mount Sinai, who died in 605, *pray for us.*

All you holy confessors, *pray for us.*

St. Mary of Egypt, who died in 421, *pray for us.*

St. Genevieve, virgin of Paris, who died in 512, *pray for us.*

St. Clotilde, queen of France, who died in 545, *pray for us.*

St. Scholastica, virgin and religions founder, who died in 543, *pray for us.*

St. Radegund, queen in Poitiers, who died in 586, *pray for us.*

All you holy virgins and holy women, *pray for us.*

All you saints of God, *intercede for us.*

Lamb of God who takes away the sins of the world, *spare us, O Lord.*

Lamb of God who takes away the sins of the world, *graciously hear us, O Lord.*

Lamb of God who takes away the sins of the world, *have mercy on us.*

Christ listen to us. *Christ hear us.*

• *Lord, you have redeemed us to God by your blood.*

• *And you have made us kings for the glory of our God.*

Let Us Pray

We ask you, Lord, by virtue of the Holy Cross of your Son, to grant our souls the grace to completely turn to you, so that burning with the fire of your love nothing in us is marked by the concupiscence of carnal or worldly desires, so it is reformed by you as a model of your sacrifice. We ask this through Jesus Christ our Lord. *Amen.*

Litany to Saints & Royals from the Middle Ages

(translated from 1600s French prayer)

Lord have mercy on us.

Christ have mercy on us.

Lord have mercy on us.

Christ have mercy on us.

Christ hear us.

O God who are the Holy of Holies, *have mercy on us.*

Blessed Virgin Mary, Mother of God, *pray for us.*

All you angels & archangels, *pray for us.*

St. Job, *pray for us.*

St. Hosea, *pray for us.*

The Holy Maccabees, *pray for us.*

All you holy patriarchs & holy prophets, *pray for us.*

St. Simon, *pray for us.*

St. Thaddeus, *pray for us.*

St. Matthias, *pray for us.*

All you holy apostles and holy evangelists, *pray for us.*

St. Anastasius, monk of Persia & companion martyrs, who died in 628, *pray for us.*

Pope St. Martin, of Rome, who died in 654, *pray for us.*

St. Prix, evangelist & Bishop of Clermont, who died in 698, *pray for us.*

St. Leger, evangelist of Autun & martyr, who died in 678, *pray for us.*

St. Boniface, evangelist of Mainz, who died in 755, *pray for us.*

St. Steven the younger & his

martyr companions, who died in Constantinople in 767, *pray for us.*

St. George & St. Aurelius martyrs of Spain, who died in 852, *pray for us.*

St. Eulogius of Cordova, priest & his martyr companions, who died in Spain in 859, *pray for us.*

St. Thomas Becket, evangelist of Canterbury, who died in 1170, *pray for us.*

St. Peter of Verona, who died in Milan in 1252, *pray for us.*

All you holy martyrs, *pray for us.*

Pope St. Gregory I (the Great), Doctor of the Church, who died in 604, *pray for us.*

St. Augustine, Archbishop of Canterbury & Apostle of the English, who died in 604, *pray for us.*

St. John, almsgiver & Patriarch of Alexandria, who died in 620, *pray for us.*

St. Loup, Archbishop of Sens, who died in 623, *pray for us.*

St. Bertrand, Bishop of Le Mans, who died in 624, *pray for us.*

St. Isidore of Seville, Doctor of the Church, who died in 636, *pray for us.*

St. Romain, Bishop of Rouen, who died in 639, *pray for us.*

St. Arnulf, Bishop of Metz, who died in 641, *pray for us.*

St. Eloy, Bishop of Noyen-Tournai, who died in 660, *pray for us.*

St. Ildephonsus, Bishop of Toledo, who died in 667, *pray for us.*

St. Faro, Bishop of Meaux, who died in 675, *pray for us.*

St. Amand, Bishop of Maestricht, who died in 684, *pray for us.*

St. Claude, Bishop of Besancon, who died in 698, *pray for us.*

St.   Tarasius,   Patriarch   of

Constantinople, who died in 806, *pray for us.*

St. Ignatius, Patriarch of Constantinople, who died in 877, *pray for us.*

St. Ulrich, Bishop of Augsburg, who died in 973, *pray for us.*

St. Dunstan, Archbishop of Canterbury, who died in 988, *pray for us.*

St. Anselm, Archbishop of Canterbury, who died in 1109, *pray for us.*

St. Godfrey, Bishop of Amiens & confessor, who died in 1118, *pray for us.*

St. Hugh, Bishop of Grenoble, who died in 1132, *pray for us.*

St. Norbert, Archbishop of Magdeburg, who died in 1134, *pray for us.*

St. Malachy, Archbishop of Armagh

& confessor, who died in 1148, *pray for us.*

St. Anthelm, Bishop of Belley, who died in 1178, *pray for us.*

St. Lawrence O'Toole, Archbishop of Dublin & confessor, who died in 1180, *pray for us.*

St. William, Archbishop of Bourges & confessor, who died in 1209, *pray for us.*

St. Edmund, Archbishop of Canterbury, who died in 1240, *pray for us.*

St. Bonaventure, Bishop of Albano, Cardinal & Doctor of the Church, who died in 1274, *pray for us.*

Pope St. Peter Celestine, confessor, who died in 1296, *pray for us.*

St. Charles Borromeo, Archbishop of Milan & Cardinal, who died in 1584, *pray for us.*

All you holy bishops, *pray for us.*

St. Columbanus, abbot of Luxeuil, who died in 615, *pray for us.*

St. Eustace, abbot of Luxeuil who died in 625, *pray for us.*

St. Gall, abbot of Arbone in Germany, who died in 646, *pray for us.*

St. Victor the Hermit, priest of Arcis-sur-Aube who died in 650, *pray for us.*

St. Fiacre, monk & hermit of Meux, who died in 670, *pray for us.*

St. Bertin, abbot of Sithieu, who died in 709, *pray for us.*

St. Bede, abbot of England, Doctor of the Church & confessor, who died in 735, *pray for us.*

St. Leufroy, abbot of the Diocese of Evreux, who died in 738, *pray for us.*

St. John of Damascus, who died in 749, *pray for us.*

St. Romuald, abbot of Ravenna, who died in 1027, *pray for us.*

*"St. Stephen I, king of Hungary, offers his crown
to the Blessed Virgin Mary" by Gyula Benczúr
(1901). Courtesy Wikimedia Commons.*

St. Stephen, king of Hungary & confessor, who died in 1038, *pray for us.*

St. Odilo, abbot of Cluny, who died in 1048, *pray for us.*

St. Edward, king of England & confessor, who died in 1066, *pray for us.*

St. Bruno of Cologne, who died in 1101, *pray for us.*

St. Robert, abbot of Molesme, who died in 1110, *pray for us.*

St. Stephen Harding, abbot of Citeaux, who died in 1134, *pray for us.*

St. Bernard, abbot of Clairvaux, who died in 1153, *pray for us.*

St. Dominic, confessor, who died in 1221, *pray for us.*

St. Francis of Assisi, who died in 1226, *pray for us.*

St. Anthony of Padua, who died in

1231, *pray for us.*

St. Louis, king of France, who died in 1270, *pray for us.*

St. Thomas Aquinas, who died in 1274, *pray for us.*

St. Elzear, Count of Ariano in Italy, who died in 1323, *pray for us.*

St. Roch, of Italy, who died in 1327, *pray for us.*

St. Vincent Ferrer, confessor, who died in 1419, *pray for us.*

St. Francis of Paola, confessor, who died in 1508, *pray for us.*

All you holy confessors, *pray for us.*

St. Fara, virgin & abbess of Faremoutier, who died in 655, *pray for us.*

St. Aurea, virgin & abbess of Paris, who died in 656, *pray for us.*

St. Gertrude, virgin & abbess of Nievelle, who died in 659, *pray for us.*

St. Bathilde, queen of France, who died in 680, *pray for us.*

St. Aldegonde, virgin & abbess of Hainault, who died in 684, *pray for us.*

St. Cunegund, Holy Roman Empress, who died in 1040, *pray for us.*

St. Hildegarde, virgin & abbess of Bingen, who died in 1179, *pray for us.*

St. Elizabeth, princess of Hungary, who died in 1231, *pray for us.*

St. Hedwig, widow & duchess of Poland, who died in 1243, *pray for us.*

St. Lutgarde, nun of Brabant, who died in 1246, *pray for us.*

St. Claire of Assisi, who died in 1253, *pray for us.*

St. Catherine of Siena, who died in Rome in 1380, *pray for us.*

St. Theresa of Avila, who died in Spain in 1584, *pray for us.*

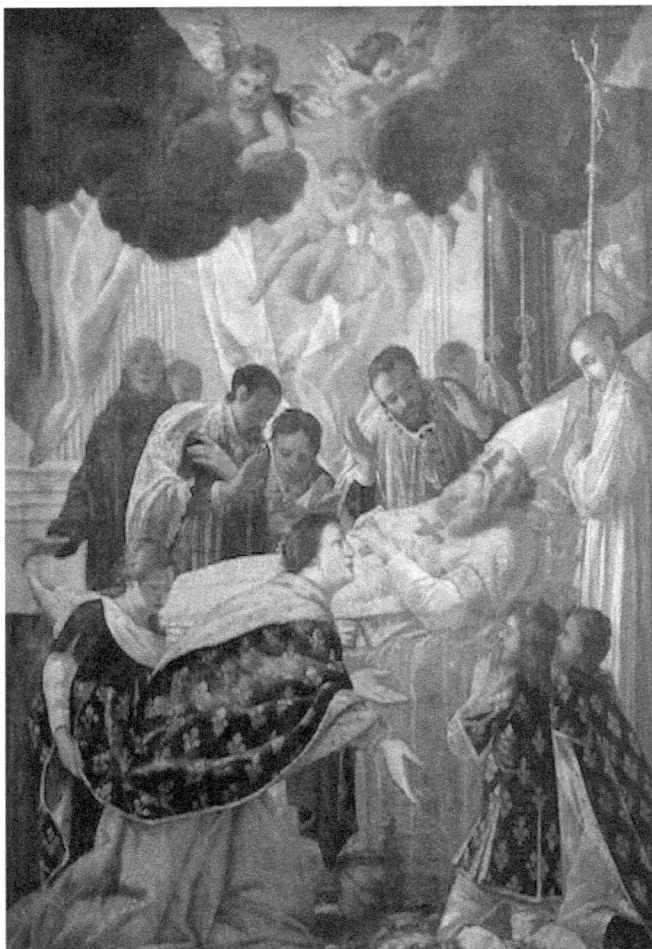

"*St. Bathilde, queen of France, at the feet of dying St. Eloy*" *by Jean Senelle: (1648). Courtesy Wikimedia Commons.*

All you holy virgins & holy women, *pray for us.*

All you saints of God, *intercede for us.*

Lamb of God who takes away the sins of the world, *spare us, O Lord.*

Lamb of God who takes away the sins of the world, *graciously hear us, O Lord.*

Lamb of God who takes away the sins of the world, *have mercy on us.*

- *Christ hear us.*

- *Christ graciously hear us.*

Let Us Pray

Receive O Lord, with favor our humble prayers, and grant us through the intercession of the Blessed Virgin Mary and of all your saints, that by virtue of your grace we may be humble in prosperity, and praise you in adversity, Lord. We ask this through Jesus Christ our Lord. *Amen.*

References

Photographs

All photos in this book were taken by Marie Noël during her visits to historic Catholic churches.

Chapter Quotations

Chapter 1: "Homily of Holy Mass for the Solemnity of Christ the King" by Archbishop Gerhard Ludwig Müller, Prefect of the Congregation for the Doctrine of the Faith (Nov. 25, 2012).

Chapter 2: "Liturgical Memorial of the Blessed Virgin Mary" by Pope Benedict XVI, General Audience (Aug. 22, 2012).

Chapter 3: "Homily, Beatification of Five Servants of God" by Pope John Paul II (Oct. 3, 2004).

Chapter 4: "Address, Vigil with Young People" by Pope Benedict XVI, during Apostolic Journey to Germany (Sept. 24, 2011).

Finis

Soli Deo Gloria

About the Author: Marie Noël

Marie Noël is an ordinary person living an ordinary life. Her love of Catholicism, interests in history, and quest to deepen her faith have led her to share this collection of prayers.

Visit her website, Facebook page, or Twitter for information on her latest prayer collections. She regularly posts historic prayers & images there.

www.booksbynoel.com
Twitter: BooksByNoel
Facebook: http://on.fb.me/YK9XOq

.

Other Prayer Collections by Marie Noël

Catholic Prayers to the King & Queen of Heaven...with prayers for kings & queens on Earth

From as old as the 11th century, the 30 select prayers are historical Catholic prayers to Jesus, Christ the King and to Mary, the Queen of Heaven, along with those to saints who were holy kings and queens.

Many prayers and litanies date back to the earliest days of the Church and were translated from various languages including French and German. This collection contains many prayers not commonly found elsewhere.

It is illustrated with beautiful color photos as well as European paintings of the saintly kings and queens from the Middle Ages.

Trade Paperback available: at bookstores, Amazon, Barnes & Noble

EBooks Available everywhere: for Kindle, the Nook, iPad & More

CATHOLIC PRAYERS
OF THANKS

Adapted & Compiled from Approved Sources
BY MARIE NOEL

Catholic Prayers of Thanks

This collection of prayers represents a year's worth of research, dating mostly from the late 1700s through the 1800s, into the Catholic history. The 60+ prayers featured are grouped as prayers of thanks:

• *To God, Jesus Christ, the Holy Spirit, the Trinity, and the Blessed Sacrament;*

- *Regarding the Church sacraments such as Mass and Confession;*

- *For each day and special occasions (your birthday, on becoming a mother, etc.); and*

- *For favors granted.*

It is illustrated with beautiful color photos as well as European religious paintings and drawings from the Renaissance. This collection offers prayers of varying lengths for convenience with the eBook readers.

Trade Paperback available: at bookstores, Amazon, Barnes & Noble

EBooks Available everywhere: for Kindle, the Nook, iPad & More

Catholic Christmas Prayers

This collection of prayers represents a year's worth of research, dating mostly from the late 1700s through the 1800s, into the Catholic history. Here are 20+ prayers, including Novenas and Litanies, in categories such as:

- *For Advent;*

- *To the Christ Child;*

- *For Christmas Eve and Christmas Day; and*

- *For Epiphany.*

It is illustrated with beautiful color photos as well as European religious paintings and drawings from the Renaissance. This collection offers prayers of varying lengths for convenience with the eBook readers.

Trade Paperback available: at bookstores, Amazon, Barnes & Noble

EBooks Available everywhere: for Kindle, the Nook, iPad & More